SURVIVING THE TECHNOLOGICAL SOCIETY

The Layman's Guide to Media Ecology

Rachel Armamentos   Brock Lockenour

"What happens if we place a drop of red dye into a beaker of clear water?" asked media ecologist Neil Postman. "Do we have clear water plus a spot of red dye? Obviously not. We have a new coloration to every molecule of water. That is what I mean by ecological change. A new medium does not add something; it changes everything."

Fish aren't often conscious of the water in which they swim—and man is no different. Too often environments with rapidly advancing technology and ever-changing media is received passively by most of society. There's a dissonance, then: the ecosystem in which we reside has a massive effect on us, and though we feel the effects we can't seem to name the cause. In order to better understand ourselves and how we interact with others, we must also understand the present world in which we live—we live in a technological society. This book is a guide to the field of research that answers that question—media ecology.

This book is about technology, media, humans, and the environment those three things create. This guide is intended for you: the mom, the pastor, the student, the professor, the curious passerby. Welcome to the land of the awake.

DEFINING THE TECHNOLOGICAL SOCIETY

Uncovering technique's impact on humankind.

BEEP BEEP BEEP—

Man jolts awake to the sound of his alarm. Disoriented at dawn, he swings his legs over the side of the bed and begins his day full of predetermined choices.

"Technique refers to any complex of standardized means for attaining a predetermined result."

Man alone cannot move at 60 miles per hour, so he crouches into his car and speeds off to work. He discontentedly crunches numbers and negotiates deals for faceless companies. He feels deadened to his position, wondering what the meaning is of his anxious hours.

On his drive home, his attention is assaulted by billboard advertisements and flippant bumper stickers. The radio fills his ears with the new chart-topper—until he grows annoyed with its repetition and connects his pre-made playlist to the car speakers.

Man arrives at home—only to disappear. In seeking freedom, he loosens his necktie, kicks off his strict shoes, and turns on the television. He is "led straight into an artificial paradise." Although he sits in the same room as his family, his body is the only sign of his presence. He is mesmerized by the pixels which

soothe a greater reality. He desires what has been curated for his viewing pleasure—financial success, sexual domination and extreme happiness. He adopts the character's successes until the program is over and the next show commences. He "lives on a screen a life [he] will never live in fact."

All of this eerie cause for overstimulation now rests in one mobile device that never leaves man. This all exists comfortably in his hand. Man cannot be alone.

Jacques Ellul—sociologist, philosopher and theologian—wrote of this Technological Society in the 1950s, yet the alarming threads of a techniqued world intensely resonate today. Thanks to technique, we are living in an artificial world.

"He must adapt himself, as though the world were new, to a universe for which he was not created. He was made to go six kilometers an hour, and he goes a thousand. He was made to eat when he was hungry and to sleep when he was sleepy; instead, he obeys a clock. He was made to have contact with living things, and he lives in a world of stone... The world that is being created by the accumulation of technical means is an artificial world and hence radically different from the natural world."

This is a Technological Society.

"The term technique, as I use it, does not mean machines, technology, or this or that procedure for attaining an end. In our technological society, technique is the totality of methods rationally arrived at and having absolute efficiency (for a given stage of development) in every field of human activity."

"Just as hydroelectric installations take waterfalls and lead them into conduits, so the technical milieu absorbs the natural." -Jacques Ellul in *The Technological Society.*

"The world that is being created by the accumulation of technical means is an artificial world and hence radically different from the natural world. It destroys, eliminates, or subordinates the natural world" - Also Jacques Ellul in *The Technological Society.*

French sociologist, philosopher, and lay theologian Jacques Ellul (1912-1994) wrote *The Technological Society*—a carefully detailed critique of technique proliferated in technology's effects on society. Written specifically throughout the pre-digital era in the 1950s, Ellul's masterpiece is applicable to modern man today. With each historical event, human activity, and analysis of machine included in his rich explanation, Ellul painstakingly describes how technique has infiltrated every aspect of society—"technique can leave nothing untouched." Ellul breaks down the activities and structure of our world—amusement and sport, for example—to reveal the technique which has invasively altered each structure. This perspective is especially understandable in the media ecological view of media as environment.

Ellul makes clear that since technique has infiltrated every aspect of society, man is also included in its path: "When technique enters into every area of life, including the human, it ceases to be external to man and becomes his very substance."

Technique as Killer of Beauty: Separation from the Aesthetic
Naturally, man is drawn to beauty, yet technique is separated from aesthetics. Ellul writes of the people's reaction to prevalent rational technique implemented in the 1880s, "It was felt that not only the traditions but the deepest instincts of humankind had been violated." In response, society created stylish decorations added to the machines as a measure bringing back aesthetics. Mechanical flowers were attached to sewing machines and engraved bulls' heads to tractors. However, technique refused these human aesthetics. Ellul writes, "an embellishment could increase air resistance, throw a wheel out of balance, alter velocity or precision. There was no room in practical activity for gratuitous aesthetic preoccupations. The two had to be separated." Technique is the infiltrator of society, the changer of man, and the killer of aesthetic beauty.

Awareness
"The negative effects come to light only many years after the product is on the market and there can be no going back. Automobiles cause terrible slaughter (12,000 deaths a year in France), but this does not halt our love affair with them." -Ellul, *The Technological Bluff.*

Oftentimes, the effects of the technology, intended or unintended, are hidden. This is because technique is covertly invasive, like propaganda. As Ellul puts it, "propaganda must become as natural as air or food... the individual is then able to declare in all

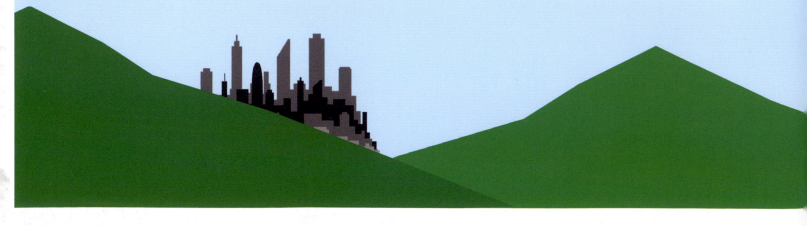

honesty that no such thing as propaganda exists. In fact, however, he has been so absorbed by it that he is literally no longer able to see the truth." In a technological society, man is never alone with his thoughts—he no longer knows how to think alone.

Society is fascinated by the idea of what technology merely can do for the person as a service to make life more efficient and easier. Enchanted, man does not consider the effect the new technology will surely have on him as well. To this point, Ellul writes in *The Technological Bluff*, "the advantages are concrete but the disadvantages are usually abstract."

For example, in *The Technological Bluff*, Ellul depicts a scenario where motorcyclists are pleased with their engines, especially when they emit maximum noise. However, it is also understood that noise presents consequences to the health of society such as issues in hearing, heart, and the nerves. Ellul writes, "in spite of its confirmed effects, which are precise and concrete, the danger seems to be an abstract one to the public."

The world today has become artificial because of technique. Man must look around to see the ugly roots of technique embedded within society. In deep consideration of technique's historical, current, and future implications, man assesses. Since man is human, man must resist technique's power of dehumanization.

In the final words of Ellul's foreword to *The Technological Society*, he hauntingly suggests the purpose of the book: "to arouse the reader to an awareness of technological necessity and what it means. It is a call to the sleeper to awake."

Jacques Ellul

Throughout *The Technological Society*, Ellul writes of the overwhelming ways in which technique has made itself present in society. Technique has situated itself in "every activity—intellectual, artistic, moral." Yet, these facets of technique in society are not often recognized or understood by the very people associated with them. Below are some beginning points of attention.

Amusement

The technological man is so driven by technique in nearly every facet of society that success is efficiency. Tainted by technique, man becomes more artificial than natural. Overwhelmed with this constant bombardment of dissociation, man finds respite by escaping into the screen. The movie theatre, his home television, his smartwatch, digital tablet, and smartphone are where man goes to "live on the screen a life [he] will never live in fact." Ellul writes that this is where the technological man finds his phantom. "The movies and television lead him straight into an artificial paradise." On the screen, man projects himself into the characters he sees displayed before him, "full of the possibilities [he] experienced in the shadows."

Education

On the technique of education, Ellul writes, "Education will no longer be an unpredictable and exciting adventure in human enlightenment, but an exercise in conformity and an apprenticeship to whatever gadgetry is useful in a technical world." Today, does education produce specialized technicians, or students who are prone to wonder at life's curiosities?

Sport

On a Sunday afternoon in the fall, enthusiastic American football fans can be seen sporting their favorite team's colors all across the country. Regardless of socio-economic standing, fans of all backgrounds cheer and watch as their team plays against rival teams. Sports bring people together, but rarely is the underlying technical form considered.

When sport becomes mechanized, it "is accompanied by the mechanization of sporting goods—stopwatches, starting machines and so on." Consider the laundry list of expensive equipment and apparel required to engage in today's sports such as specialized cleats, matching uniforms, regulation size and weight balls, different running shoes for the stability on a free and wild trail, or a more cushioned run with memory foam inserts on a rubberized track.

In terms of the players themselves, Ellul suggests, "training in sports makes of the individual an efficient piece of apparatus which is henceforth unacquainted with anything but the harsh joy of exploiting his body and winning." Here, Ellul explains that instead of being enjoyed as activity, with technique, sport becomes technical with adherence to strict rules, set boundaries, and a near always goal of winning.

"The world that is being created by the accumulation of technical means is an artificial world and hence radically different from the natural world."

- The Technological Society

Vacation

Have you ever returned from a vacation more exhausted, and wished you could have another vacation just to recuperate? There may be a reason for this. In 1938, Billy Butlin created "family vacation camps;" self contained entertainment villages where organized activities were scheduled from early in the morning until late in the evening. In describing the atmosphere, Butlin mentioned of his camps, "the important thing is that no one is ever left to himself even for a moment." Of these planned vacations, Ellul writes, "everything takes place in a spirit of gaiety and liveliness and under the direction of game leaders who are 'specialists.' All available means are employed to persuade the individual that he is happy."

How much of advertised vacations consist of constant activity to get the most out of money spent—how much is an actual break? Similarly, the individual living in the technological society works and saves money for 48 weeks a year to receive four weeks of vacation in which case he can spend it on once in a lifetime, life-giving experience which make him feel more human.

Sleep

Ellul suggests that machines create new environments and alter man: "He must adapt himself... He was made to go six kilometers an hour, and he goes a thousand. He was made to eat when he was hungry and to sleep when he was sleepy; instead, he obeys a clock."

Studies show that to view a digital screen—computer, tablet, smartphone—before going to bed is changing the way humans sleep and function the next day. Psychology professor at California State University Larry Rosen writes, the "blue wavelength light from LED-based devices increases the release of cortisol in the brain, which makes us more alert, and inhibits the production of melatonin, which is needed to fall asleep." Contrary to their known health detriments, these screens are often some of the last things man views before falling asleep. Yet again a technology impedes that which is natural as part of man's new routine in the technological society.

Dr. Read Mercer Schuchardt

With an M.A. and a Ph.D in Media Ecology from New York University, Dr. Read Mercer Schuchardt is one of the leading minds in a theologically informed media ecology. He is an Associate Professor of Communication at Wheaton College, co-author of *Understanding Jacques Ellul*, and co-founder of *Second Nature* online journal of technology and Christianity. He and his wife Rachel have ten children.

What is the "Technological Society?"

RMS: The "Technological Society" is the term given to modern life in the 20th century by Jacques Ellul, the French sociologist from the University of Bordeaux in 1954. What Ellul was pointing out was the technology was now the dominant factor in understanding society and structures and organizational patterns and also the dominant force that had taken on a spiritual force of its own and man had to reckon with in order to survive as a spiritual being.

Why is a study of the technological society important today?

RMS: In 1954 when Ellul wrote this, people didn't quite get it, and they thought he was being hyperbolic or overstating the case and that was of course as we move from a mechanical age into an electronic age. So in 1954 when television wasn't even yet a mass medium, it must have seemed like quite an overstatement. The digital revolution started in 1990, the Internet became a mass medium in 1997, and social media and the smartphone became a mass medium in 2007, meaning that we have now been in digital society for 11 years. It's more important than ever because the society we live in now is sort of a technological society 3.0 where it is electronic plus digital, plus now what we are seeing is the convergence of all digital media. So to understand the effects—the neurological effects, the psychological effects, the environmental effects, the human cultural organizational effects, the religious effects—you have to study it with nuance more carefully and subtly than ever before to understand the world in which you live in. So, if the study of history is important to know the past in order to know where you came from and where you are going, then the study of technological history is the primary mechanism in which you hold onto your identity, your history, and your sanity in the 21st century.

What would you suggest to the layman who is interested (with hesitancy) to study Jacques Ellul's "The Technological Society?"

RMS: Every student should study Ellul and *The Technological Society* as well as the larger school and discipline of media ecology that he helped found because media and the environment it creates—the ecology of media—is in fact the world we live in. It is in fact the water we swim in. When you consider that we spend 12 of our 16 waking hours in mass media every day, to not understand the origin, history, nature, trajectory, and purpose of the media is to literally be completely ignorant of one's surroundings. If you go to bed with your iPhone and you wake up with your iPhone and all day you are touching, swiping and pinching your iPhone 2,500 times a day, which is the average, then you have to understand what that does to you, what it is doing to you, and what recourse you have to resist its unintended consequences. So even if it is not your major or your discipline you want to study for knowledge's sake, it is something you should always be paying careful attention to just to live well and just to be able to thrive in a 1.75 million app universe.

What looks differently between the technological society from the 1950s and now?

RMS: The biggest difference is that it is a move from the electronic world to the digital world. And that is primarily a difference of discrete technologies, where you had a toaster that was a technology you plugged in and turned on and that's all it did was toast your bread. You had a radio and you turned it on and turned it off, and it just played the radio stations. They were all discrete technologies with their own little plug. Digital technologies takes all those technologies and converges them so now you can buy an alarm clock that wakes you up with your favorite song and toasted bread for breakfast in one machine. When your technologies converge like that, it means it becomes impossible to not participate in the technological system and society in order to get anything done. Everybody knows that Alexa is spying on you, and based on what you are saying, is feeding you ads now based on acoustic speech to text and text to speech software and algorithms, but at the same time, it is harder and harder to live without a smart speaker in your home because more and more that is all they sell now at the stores. As technology progresses, you can't go back and choose the old technologies. You could choose to hold on to your old analog black and white television set, but if you plug it in and turn it on, you'll just get a snow screen. You won't get any channels because all the channels of transmission now are transmitting on a digital frequency signal. My old blender and my old toaster still work, but in terms of communication technology, once it goes digital, you have no choice but to go backwards. Even in some of them like the rebirth of vinyl in 2015 where vinyl surpassed digital music sales, that is a form of nostalgia that is itself kind of co-opted by the technological digital system. When I buy Leonard Cohen's last album on vinyl, I am also getting the digital code for an MP3 download, and I am playing it on a turntable, but it is through a digital system and if I want, I can have it play on all the speakers in my house and rip it from vinyl to my iTunes library because it is all digitally transferrable in seconds. There is a sort of ubiquity, convergence and inevitability that digital technology presents us that is somewhat inescapable. If kids today need an iPad just to get through 3rd grade, that tells you how necessary and inevitable it is.

What is technique?
RMS: By technique Ellul means the one best way of doing something and achieving an end, and by the one best way he means an absolute slavery to a definition of efficiency that achieves its ends by dividing and conquering a sequence of events into discrete and repeatable units that may separate that which God may have put together. Technique, at the end of the day is a divide and conquer scheme, spiritually speaking, which is dividing and separating that which was once inseparable. By breaking things up into discrete units, we now think we have control and the ability to guide their destiny when in fact separation of that which God intended is destroying our ability to remember what we are doing, why we are here, and what it is we are doing in the first place. It is not a coincidence that the technological system has produced the most tech savvy generation ever in the history of the world, at the same time it has produced the most anxious, depressed, and suicidal generation in the history of the world. While technology disembodies us, as one of the ultimate seven vices of the virtual life as I call it, that disembodiment is a technologically driven form of the ancient heresy of gnosticism, so it is also no surprise that the world's most technological society that has now gone global is also the same historical epic in which we are seeing the greatest resurgence of the rise and rebirth and renaissance of gnosticism itself. The idea that the spirit is good and matter is evil is just the opposite of the Christian Incarnational message of Christ, which is that matter matters, and the body is the temple of the spirit—the two are not separable. One of the ultimate demonic effects of technique is that it separates the mind from the body or the spirit from the body in the way that God put them together. By disconnecting body and spirit, we are literally out of joint with ourselves and we don't know who we are, where we are going, or why we are here.

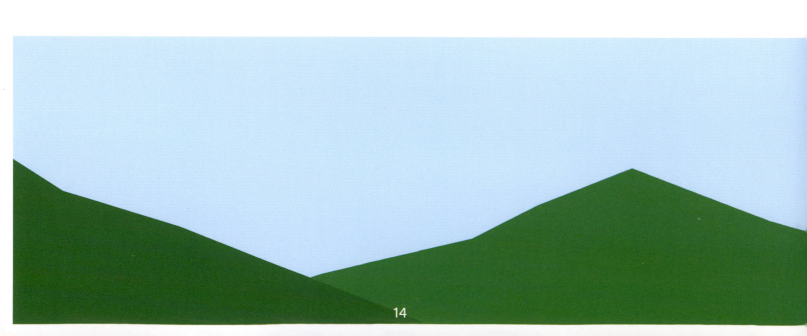

What is the answer? What can be done?

RMS: The answer is Jesus. What can be done is cling closer to Jesus and pray without ceasing. In order to combat the spiritual deadening effects of technology and technological gadgetry, which are the unintended effects, then you have to displace it with something. So, clinging to Christ and understanding Christ as the logos, as the original source and code of information in the universe of the pre-existing spiritual information that codes all biological systems, all chemical systems, all neural synapse information transfer systems and all systems of hierarchy and meaning making that humans are capable of—that is important, and Scripture's answer is pray without ceasing. In a sense, prayer is the only way you can dispell and keep at bay the creeping effect of a 12 hour a day mass media digital tech habit. Prayer is really a form of communication. We are starting to understand that this is return to origins where this technology already existed in a pre-digital age and it was simply called prayer. I think we are on the cusp of a fantastic new revolutionary series of perceptions where we understand the old tools and techniques and tricks that God gave us to survive and thrive in planet earth are in fact precisely the things we need to survive and thrive now. It is very interesting that the National Day for Unplugging, for instance, is led mostly by Jewish tech scholars, tech pundits and tech workers who understand that we need a Sabbath—we need one day a year that we don't do this, where we are free from our technological addiction and our technological slavery. This is in fact key to human happiness and survival in a technological age. In the same way that the regular Sabbath takes you out of the cycle of work and getting and spending in the service of mammon in the old sense, so too does the technological Sabbath on a daily, weekly and yearly basis, break the enthrallment, or spell, or binding power of that system to slavery. So, to become aware of the need for a form of spiritual resistance is to become spiritually alive. Jacques Ellul said that existence is resistance—"l'existence est resistance." By that Ellul meant you have to be aware of it before you can know where to fight back, where to resist, and where to offer your time and energy in a different direction.

As to what can be done? Individuals can act, communities can act, churches can act, groups can act collectively. I think it would be amazing if people came to think of Christians the way they did in the ancient world. These are the people who don't bow to Caesar in the ancient world; they go to the gladiator's rings and get fed to the lions and sing while doing so. If we were known in the 21st century as people that are sane in a digitally insane world, as people who can make eye contact and shake hands and enjoy human empathy in conversation and share the delivery and transmission and reception of serotonin and dopamine with each other rather than through our devices, then I think people would go, "oh, they've actually got something that they are offering that is real, quantifiable, and that I need and that I want." To make the connection between that and Christian theology I think would be a profound opportunity.

THE MEDIUM IS THE MESSAGE

How the tech that carries a message may be more important than the content.

Marshall McLuhan

Star Wars was released in theaters on May 25th, 1977. The boomers and their parents heard the buzz around the flick and waited hours in line, then crammed into their seats next to neighbors to experience this galaxy far far away. Minds were blown, and fanatical Star Wars fans were made that day in droves.

Twenty years later, their kids first watched Star Wars—but it was different. Rather than cinemas with large screens and booming sound crowded with eager communities, they experienced a different environment: living rooms. Usually at the urging of their nostalgic dad, these kids first met Luke, Han, and Leia from the worn seats of their couch, the same place they sit bored with relatives after eating Thanksgiving turkey.

Kids of today who watch Star Wars probably first saw the yellow title crawl on their iPad sitting in their bedroom, or alone in their family room.

Obviously, the original viewers of Star Wars got a wholly different experience than their kids who watched the same movie in the early 90's. Everyone has a 'first-time' story with Star Wars, but the impact just isn't the same from generation to generation.

There's a reason Star Wars seems much more monumental for older generations. It's because the medium that transmitted the message was different.

Medium:
one of the means or channels of general communication, information, or entertainment in society, such as newspapers, radio, or television.

Message:
a communication containing some information, news, advice, request, or the like.

Marshall McLuhan, Canadian professor, philosopher and media ecologist, writes, "the medium is the message. This is merely to say that the personal and social consequences of any medium—that is, of any extension of ourselves—result from the new scale that is introduced into our affairs by each extension of ourselves, or by any new technology."

There are two components to any message: 1) the content (the message) and 2) the form (the medium). The content of the message is what is held by the form that the message is communicated through.

McLuhan states that the message emitted by the medium has little to do with what is actually received and processed by the receiver. Rather, the medium itself has a greater impact on the receiver. In this way, the medium is the message.

McLuhan uses an example of the technology of the manufacturing machine to explain this idea. He states "Many people would be disposed to say that it was not the machine, but what one did with the machine, that was its meaning or message. In terms of the ways in which the machine altered our relations to one another and to ourselves; it mattered not in the least whether it turned out cornflakes or Cadillacs. The restructuring of human work and association was shaped by the technique of fragmentation that is the essence of machine technology."

So what does this mean—both as a concept, and as something we should pay meticulous attention to apply in our own lives?

For example, let's say you are in a long distance relationship and you and your significant other want a way to stay in communication while you are spatially separated. Do you think that communication is better held under conditions of digital social mediums or through handwritten letters delivered through the mail? Which form means more?

Certainly the paper letter that has been handwritten and shaped by your loved one means something different than a text delivered on a screen. A text on a cell phone means something different than a handwritten letter regardless of the content. The message could read the same on the cell phone as it reads in the handwritten letter, but the form of the content sends a message itself.

You may think, why does this form of communication mean more to me? The answer: it carries a bias and a meaning behind it. While personal meaning will vary between individuals, there is a certain universal bias to the communication form.

A cell phone has a technological bias to signify individualistic functions, while a handwritten letter signifies a thoughtful and careful gesture.

This method also applies in interpersonal communication. Imagine that you need to tell your friend some exciting news—you landed your dream job! You meet, and as you begin to speak, your friend's phone vibrates to signify an incoming text message. Her eyes flitter away from you to look at the message. This action tells you that her focus is elsewhere—no longer on you and your exciting news.

The way in which one listens actually communicates incredible (and often lasting) messages to the speaker. This can be found in a daily and close study of one's own speaking and listening skills since both have such powerful implications for personal and interpersonal transformation.

Understanding this, we therefore strive to be good stewards of our communications skills through components of listening, especially hearing, attending, understanding, remembering, and responding. Arguably, the most relevant (and unfortunately absent) facet of listening today is attending. This is a psychological and physical part of the listening process. Today, much of interpersonal communication has been completed through digitalized mediums, often through social media. However, social media (and most digital communication) requires its user to be physically absent from their current physical environment in order to communicate with the party on the other end of the digitized line.

For example, a teenage girl takes a Snapchat selfie and immediately uploads it to her platform of viewers to show that she is having a great time at her party. This mode of communication may seem harmless enough at first glance, but with a closer look, we notice that in order for the girl to share information to others on the other end of her phone's connection, 1) she distracts from the current company with the presence of her cell phone, 2) her mind goes elsewhere (to wherever her friend is located rather than where her body is physically located) yet her body stays at the party.

This disturbance—which is physiological, psychological, and emotional—causes dissonance as the girl is torn between two different locations and two different groups of friends. This is cause for concern for the state of this girl and her interpersonal relationships alone, however today it goes much further than the scope of this example. Our society is tethered to their personal devices which aid in the spread of this method of communication so distant from the aspect of attendance. With this comes a myriad of consequences which includes many issues with listening and responding in interpersonal relationships.

In modern Western culture, we are inundated with all sorts of technological media forms—social media, fitness tracking watches, cell phone apps to locate and navigate around police officers on the highway, and more. Often, it is believed that the way we use these devices is more important than the actual device itself.

McLuhan suggests that technology should not be considered for how it is used—that is, the function of a technology is not based around how you use it—but that it has certain inherent biases.

In *Understanding Media*, McLuhan makes his point painfully clear: "Our conventional response to all media, namely that it is how they are used that counts, is the numb stance of the technological idiot. For the 'content' of the medium is like the juicy piece of meat carried by the burglar to distract the watchdog of the mind."

If Mediums could speak:

Television

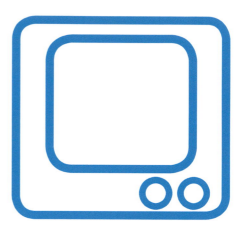

"I'm wholesome! You can watch me alone, with your family, even with your friends! Because it's easier to communally consume a big-budget program than make actual conversation, right? And after all, you organized your living room around me."

Radio

"Well why wouldn't you want to listen to this song seven times a day? It's chart topping! And hey, we'll play that song in just a minute, so don't go anywhere during the ads. And don't feel bad if your kid's in the car either, everyone else stuck in traffic is hearing the same thing."

Laptop

"Through me you have the power to explore and create in an utterly private space! This is YOUR laptop, after all. You have a right to everything here, and I'm basically essential to life now. By the way, I need an upgrade soon, and free access to information only happens because of ads."

What message do popular mediums send?

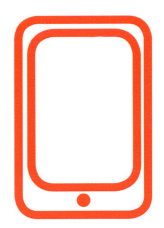

Smart Phone

"A world of information at your fingertips! You, yes, YOU are the master of your own destiny. You can do whatever you want with me! Just make sure you don't set me down. Once you taste the power you'll never want to go back. Also, I'm totally private, and texts are as urgent as personal conversation."

Movie Theater

"Let's all experience this together! Bigger is better, and we are the best way to experience something great in a community. Audience reaction is part of the excitement. Also, you'd rather pay for an experience than just a simple product, wouldn't you?"

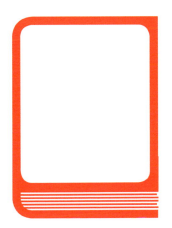

Book

"It's just you and me. You have an opinion, and what you think matters- so read me! Make sure I'm written by an author you follow. Don't forget you have the ability to flip through my chapters and skip around! My author doesn't really mind as long as you've already bought the book."

Dr. Eric McLuhan

Dr. Eric McLuhan was a leading scholar, lecturer and author in the field of media and communication theory. He was also Dr. Marshall McLuhan's son. In our conversation, he provided many rich insights on the background of the famous phrase, "the medium is the message."

Did the arrival of the TV necessitate a new lens for the topic of advertising?

EM: Every medium brings with it a completely new sensibility and a new form of culture, and it is invisible.

Most people misunderstand the phrase, "the medium is the message" completely, although my father went to great pains in *Understanding Media* to point out exactly what he meant. When he used the word "medium," he means what they mean. Between the 50s and the 60s or 70s, this word changed its meaning a lot. Responsible scholars look at dictionaries from, say, the 30s and 40s and find out what the word meant then. Then you look at dictionaries after the 50s (since TV hit in the 1950s) between 1952 and 1958, when, roughly, we went from 15% of households having TV sets to 80% of households having TV sets. The jump is enormous. Everything changed in that period; from hot to cold. The cold war was an information war. A hot war is guns and bombs, so the difference was between hardware and software. So the medium is an environment. It is not a box of tubes, it is an environment that surrounds the culture. And the content of any environment is every other environment. So when a new medium comes along, that is a new environment, and it immediately surrounds the old culture in totality. It doesn't leave anything untouched—everything gets processed, reprocessed, and reshaped.

Now, when you say, "the medium is the message," you mean all of those environmental changes are the message of the new technology. And that is what most people miss.

What would you say are some of the most prevalent misconceptions about the concept of "the medium is the message?"

EM: There isn't world enough or time to get [to cover all] those with any depth. Let's take one basic principle: When a new environment comes along and surrounds the old one, suddenly the old one appears. It has always been invisible, but the minute a new environment comes along, all the old things that used to be invisible suddenly appear. And people see it and think what they now see is the new world. It isn't. It is the old world. That is one of the basic misconceptions.

Media ecology—my father and I invented that term, by the way—came about like this: when a new medium like television comes along, let's say, or computers, it immediately starts to trash, and go to war with, all the old ones. Television went to war with radio, and also with movies—with Hollywood. The content of TV is the old processes, and what you get on TV is movies, and newspapers, and news reports, and music. What you had on radio was again, the preceding environment. But when you take it over, you reshape the old thing entirely. Lots of people who were big stars on radio tried to get on TV, but it didn't work—it never does work.

When an old thing begins to be retrieved in new patterns, then you know there is a new environment in place, and you better start looking for it.

Our idea of ecology was why let this continual warfare between forms and media take place? It is very costly, it is very disrupting, very confusing, and the culture gets rewritten or rebuilt each time. So let's apply the ecology idea to environments. The idea was to control these things—well, there is no control whatever. The minute some new form appears, who takes over but the marketers? They don't want control! The idea of ecology being applied to cultural and media environments has never really been taken seriously. But what people do try and do is control the content and the programs. That, by the way, nowadays is called literacy. TV literacy and art literacy and so on. That is one sign that actual literacy is dead.

The poet helps you see the world. When you put on the poem, you become the content. When you are watching TV or the computer screen, you are the content. And the thing you are looking at or the thing you are reading is really an excuse to soak yourself in that environment.

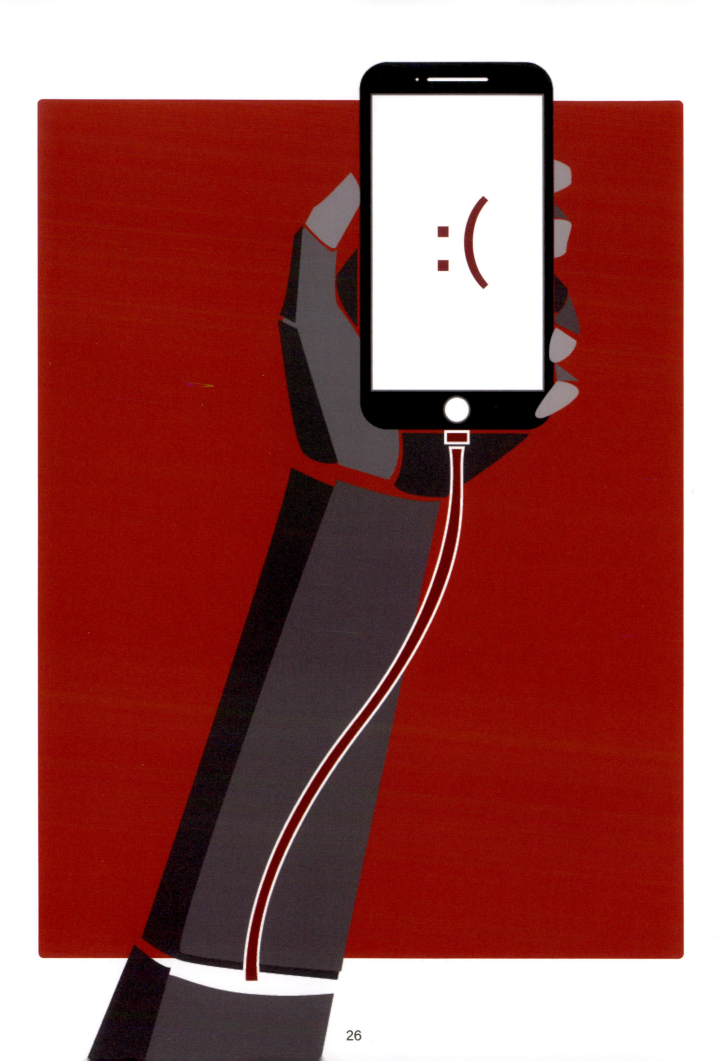

ADDICTED BY DESIGN

The empty promises of an always-connected society.

Internet is,
uh, that masive
computer network,
the one that is becoming
really big now.

"I am afraid that if I subscribe to something like Internet..." she would add in a later interview, "I would get hooked and I would never, you know, spend time with my family."

This scene, first recorded and televised in 1994, is today accessible on the very Internet Ms. Couric wanted nothing to do with all those years ago.

Viewed today, two well-known talk show hosts asking innocent, oblivious questions about 'Internet' may seem comical, but the end of the clip poses a question as relevant to modern audiences as it was in 1994.

In the words of Katie Couric, "is it worth it?"

Since 1994, the Internet has come a long way in the eyes of society. What once existed as a nebulous catch-all for 'futuristic technology' has been adopted into nearly every home in America. What was only a foreign thought only 24 years ago is now a cemented reality.

This is a technological society—are we connected, or addicted?

"The first few weeks is literally like coming off a drug," said an ex-Facebook user quoted in a 2018 Ad Age article titled *Over Sharing* "My mind was programmed to check Facebook. Even after I deleted the app, I would randomly pick up my phone and click where the app used to be, just out of habit."

According to the National Center on Addiction and Substance Abuse, "Addiction is a complex disease of the brain and body that involves compulsive use of one or more substances despite serious health and social consequences." The Hazelden Betty Ford Foundation defined technology addiction as "frequent and obsessive technology-related behavior increasingly practiced despite negative consequences to the user of the technology."

What makes the Internet so addictive? Bright, flashy and ever-refreshing, the Internet attracts the human desire for stimulation and interaction. "Technology impacts the pleasure systems of the brain in ways similar to substances. It provides some of the same reward that alcohol and other drugs might: it can be a boredom buster, a social lubricant, and an escape from reality"

Society is far too willing to overlook signs of concerning addiction to instead consider the alluring benefits of technological advancements— the smartphone is society's friend, entertainer, workout partner, matchmaker, mobile banker, and personal confidante. It took ten years for psychologist Sigmund Freud to come to terms with his addiction to the substance he considered for its initial benefits of unprecedented energy and treatment of depression. The substance? Cocaine.

If we are bored in the real, we know we can be entertained in the virtual. We do not use these technologies only to fill time when we are bored, we also use it to avoid tasks, responsibilities, and people. But the Internet as a never ending source of entertainment will never leave us bored. In fact, we do not let it leave us at all. The phone never leaves our reach—it makes comfortable habitats in pockets, on desks, and in hands.

To that extent, the mere presence of the cell phone is a message itself. A 2017 study at the University of Texas at Austin tested the effects of just the sight of a nearby smartphone on a person's ability to complete tasks. Researchers found,

"It didn't matter whether a person's smartphone was turned on or off, or whether it was lying face up or face down on a desk. Having a smartphone within sight or within easy reach reduces a person's ability to focus and perform tasks because part of their brain is actively working to not pick up or use the phone."

In another study published in the *Journal of Social and Personal Relationships*, "partners who attempted to share a meaningful conversation in the presence of a phone reported less trust than those who did so in its absence." Therefore, the sight of a smartphone in the midst of a two-person conversation lowered relationship quality, trust, and empathy.

Ponder: What does this mean for your relationships in a time when phones are always on, always nearby, and always visible?

Just like cracking your knuckles or taking a sip of water will likely influence others around you to crack their knuckles and search for their own water bottles, the mere sight of a smartphone makes it more likely that others around them will pull out their own phone.

"When society is addicted, profit is generated."

Experiment: If you are in a space with people, pull out your phone now. Don't do anything with it, just pull it out and set it on the table. Click the home button to light it up as if you are checking the time. Odds are that someone around you mimicked by checking their own device.

This is not a coincidence—when society is addicted, profit is generated.

In 2012, Facebook collected approximately $5.32 per each of their 1 billion users. In 2017, there were 2.2 billion Facebook users and the ARPU, or "average revenue per user," was $20.21. Pause. That comes out to $44,462,000,000. Keeping users on Facebook is a multi-billion dollar business. Facebook is about far more than just your connectedness—it's about their wallet.

Keeping a clear focus on how the individual's presence on the site directly correlates to revenue, the importance of design process is incredible.

Sites like Facebook are designed to create addicts. Devices 'ping' audibly, vibrate, and display flashing colorful banners across the device's home screen, all to immediately grab attention and inform the user of a notification. Professor and interruption scientist Gloria

Mark says it takes 23 minutes on average for an individual to return to an assignment after interruption. Yet, we welcome constant distractions by agreeing to notifications for every upcoming Starbucks Star Reward double-star day, Snapchat picture, ESPN score update, early morning email from the boss, Instagram mention, and BOGO deal at the mall.

Ponder: Are each of these interruptions worth an extra 23 minutes of distraction? Are they always worth the 23 minutes of the person you might be distracting on the other end of your outgoing mail?

In another familiar example of social media's systemic control by design, an individual's sense of freedom is commandeered by covert tactics to steal time. Someone watching Netflix may find themselves several episodes and hours deep into a show as a direct output of design. Think of it this way: the thrilling show frustratingly ends on a cliffhanger, but fear not, the clicking timer has predetermined the outcome of a continued binge (unless the user actively closes out of the auto-play).

Similarly, it is no coincidence that just after a video regarding a specific topic or issue is watched, videos with a like theme appear and begin to play one after the other. How? Using speech-to-text algorithms (which are given access through apps that ask "allow microphone?")—simply put, your favorite social media is listening to you. Internet sites bait users to stay longer by feeding them advertisements based off of what is searched for, clicked on, hovered over or, most eerily, spoken about in conversation.

Just as casino walls are void of clocks and windows to keep gamblers in a limbo—unaware of a sense of time—the environment of Google is also manipulated for certain feedback. Side column advertisements are based on a viewer's click history—perfectly curated material. More clicks mean more data for Google to collect and sell for profit. Almost no social media platforms require a financial cost to the consumer, which means, "If you're not paying for the product, the product is you."

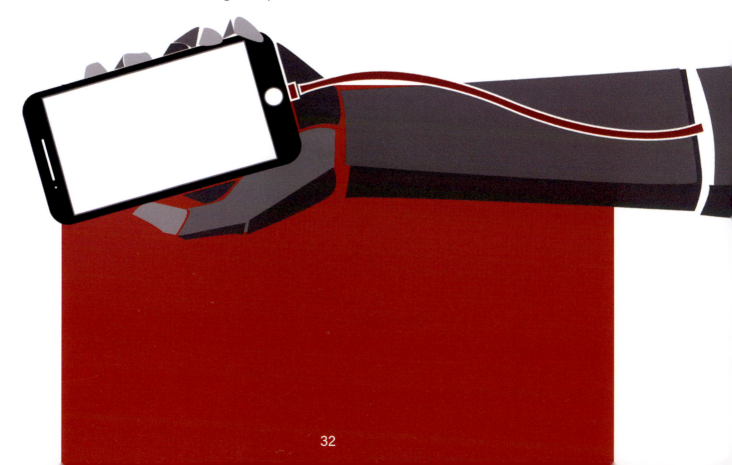

Phone Numbers

The modern world loves technology—but here's a look at some of the hard data surrounding cell phones. Addiction is an understatement.

The average Internet user spends 6 hours online each day.

95%

of Americans own a cell phone.

6-12 minutes

The average amount of time people last before checking their phone.

4 out of every 10 dollars spent online is at Amazon.

2,617

Average number of taps, swipes, and clicks per person each day.

WARNING: By the time of publication, this data is already outdated—and it's probably gotten even worse.

Eric Brende

Eric Brende—a rickshaw driver in St. Louis—holds degrees from Yale University, Washburn University, and M.I.T. In the first year of their marriage, Eric and his wife spent eighteen months living more technologically conservative than the Amish to find out how much technology is actually needed in order to live a full and happy life. Eric writes of "the best year of his life" in his book, *Better Off: Flipping the Switch on Technology.*

What do you think the smartphone does to a person in terms of their ability to communicate with others in society when the phone has become a person's community?

EB: To answer specifically, it ironically pushes people further apart. If you look at the word 'media,' it is a word for "middle." "In medias-res" is Latin for "the middle of things." What is supposed to be connecting you actually becomes a barrier instead of a conduit. It is a small slice of full face to face contact. With this technology, you can only increase the radius of contact by diluting the quality. For example, your number of Facebook friends increases, but the quality of those relationships decreases. It is terribly insidious. Addiction promises something is doesn't deliver. The more you use it, the worse you feel. And then the more you use it.

As a rickshaw driver in St. Louis, what is your response when customers choose to be on their phones instead of enjoying the ride by talking with their company, with you, or by looking at their surroundings on the ride?

EB: It is their loss. Sometimes they start talking, and I respond, and they say, "I am not talking to you"—they are on their phones. It is the least of my worries. Haven't you ever had this happen? You are at the library and then you hear, "Hello? OH HI, DEAR!" and it is about 5 times louder and completely shuts out everything around them. You could jump up and down and they would not notice.

What do you think about the quick eye glance towards a lit up phone, or the almost instinctual hand twitch when a phone vibrates—even in the middle of conversation?

EB: You are not exempt from the laws of common courtesy just because you are with your phone. It is just like when people are in traffic, it is somehow OK to be rude, but those same people would never be that rude in person.

From your unique perspective of living low tech in a digital world, how do you think we are marketed to and through our addictions?

EB: If you look at the revenue of a local tavern and talk to the tavern owner and ask him, "Don't you feel bad about contributing to alcoholism?" he will say, "No, I believe in moderate drinking." But, 80% of the tavern income revenue comes from over drinking. It's even higher at Apple, Microsoft, Amazon and Google, but they would swear up and down, "We don't believe in addiction." But their income is 99% from of people who overuse the medium, so they maximize the extent at which it is addictive. They know all the little tricks of how to do that. They have even come out with statements that they do not let their own kids use their products.

In a New York Times interview, Nick Bilton wrote, "So, your kids must love the iPad?" "They haven't used it," [Jobs] told me. "We limit how much technology our kids use at home."

What must this Internet-addicted society do to live more embodied lives in a technological world that is increasingly disembodied?

EB: The civil answer is to not use all those devices. But the more practical answer is you can cordon off those devices with limited access. For example, I have a pay-per-minute flip phone so I am aware of the minutes I am paying for. To minimize Internet access, we do not have Internet at our house and I have to walk to the library to access my email account. In other words, I have a cell phone, but not a smartphone. I have access to the Internet, but not in my house. We have bikes and the rickshaw, but not a car. We had a car for the first few years we lived in St. Louis because I thought we would need it. Even if you consciously try to limit it, you still have it on hand. Then you think, "I'll just run this one time to the store..." Then it is constant—all the time.

What would you suggest to a reader who is addicted to the Internet and might not know it, or refuses to believe it?

EB: People usually only try to resolve an addiction if they think it is a problem that affects others. Recently, my wife and I went on vacation and there was a TV with Netflix in the hotel. We thought we would watch one movie as a treat—a movie because then we would not spend all that time flipping through TV to find something. But we could not figure Netflix out, so then we went back to TV to find a program guide, but we could not find that either, so we just started scrolling. We ended up spending so much time trying to find something that we wasted all that time. It is the same thing with the Internet. It must be limited in the effect. I think about how often society uses the TV and wonder—how can they tolerate having TV on all the time? Brains are unraveling, and if they don't see it, that is a problem.

YOU BECOME WHAT YOU BEHOLD

Situating music within man.

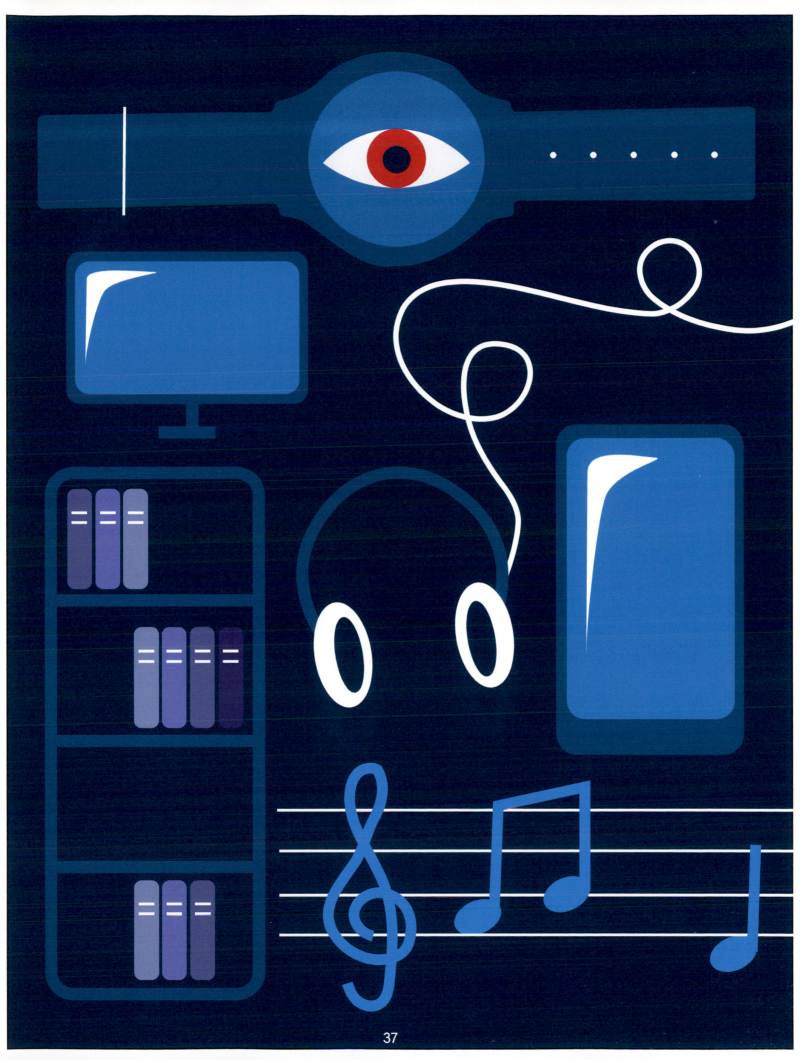

Who are you? Why are you, you?

The first answer to these questions can be summed up in one phrase: "We Become What We Behold." This idea relates closely to the phrase, 'The Medium is the Message.' In a world where evenings are spent watching television, a generation became entertainment. We thought, spoke, and lived entertainment. In today's world of beholding ourselves in selfies and social media, what are we becoming? Narcissists.

If skeptical of the idea, there's an easy example in the pages ahead. The proof is also the answer for what to behold in order to become a human that holistically lives like a human and not under the influence of machines. This example and answer is music.

When's the last time you woke up and thought that this day ahead of you could be the last you'll ever live? Doing this practice might seem morbid, but it shouldn't necessarily be. Our lives are short. To not live with this in mind, is to live half lives—lives not spurred on to urgency, and, for lack of a better term, life. Instead we live to get to the next thing.

The American rushes past the fleeting days of childhood, yearns through high school to get out into the "real world," then attends college only to get a job, then works said job to get money that never seems to mean anything. Retirement begins with only a few years left—more often than not, it is spent looking back wondering if work wasn't as bad as everyone thought it was. Life in western society is a vicious cycle of forgetfulness—of forgetting to live.

Ironically, the only way to live is by remembering death.

If "value is a function of scarcity," then the scarcest thing you've got is time, and the only way to truly know (know with your heart, head, fingers and ears) this is by keeping death before you. It's the true paradox: to become life—you must behold death. And this is death: Music.

Music is organized sounds in relation to each other in time. It's also one of the main ways to perceive the fleetingness of time. Sound is the most fleeting of all things sensed. It only exists as it's fading from existence, and it makes that fragile, dying existence sensory to us. This is important for life because this principle: YOU BECOME WHAT YOU BEHOLD.

Different mediums carry different biases. For the sake of this example, television is an easy one to pick on. Famed media ecologist Neil Postman says all content on television is entertainment meant to keep people watching and consuming as long as possible. One could know it's entertainment by watching what is included in, for example, the nightly news. There are videos sent in so the audience can be included and see interesting weather from places that won't actually affect their lives at all. Weather itself is frankly fun to watch and hear about, so every hurricane gets top story. Of course, however well-informed, no ugly anchor would land a job on screen—they're just not entertaining to watch. But the important takeaway is that as people watch (behold) the news (the entertainment) they start to speak, think and act like entertainment. We become the entertainment we behold on the television.

I know I am entertainment. How many times have I said or done something just to entertain those around me? Humans were not meant to be amusement. A-muse means to not-think. And what is it that being amusement keeps you from thinking about? Life, and how short and valuable it is. But this is good for the TV companies because if you are not aware of how little time you have left, you are probably still wasting away in front of the tube.

Not all instances of one becoming what one beholds are so sinister as the TV. This same principle actually explains why a husband and wife will look and think and act like each other after years of beholding each other in marriage.

Society becomes what society beholds as well. In any given sanctuary—especially in Protestant churches—seating is arranged in forward facing rows. It hasn't always been this way. In the Protestant Reformation in the 16th century, the book of the Bible became central in theology of Martin Luther as the all books became central in society because of the printing press. People beheld the book and the text in it, and organized the chairs in the church like the book they beheld, two columns of rows.

Modern man also thinks like the book—linearly, logically, progressively. Because of the book, eyes became the most important sense because brains received far more information through them than ever in history. Then came pictures, and now moving pictures play everywhere. The eye cannot know time like the ear, and so there exists problem—we have forgotten time in our bleary eyed lives. By forgetting time, man has forgotten how to live.

So now we can circle back to the beginning: Music. By beholding music man becomes what man truly is, a short sound, existing only while fading out of existence. This is a life conscious of scarcity—and at the same time—conscious of its value. This happens because of the way music and ears interact.

There is a coiled organ in every ear called the cochlea. If one were to unwind it and observe as music enters into it, they would see spots light up in correspondence to each specific note of music heard. The locations that light up, are in direct correspondence to the highness or lowness of the notes, so if you played a middle C on a keyboard, something like the center of the cochlea would light up. Thus the cochlea actually internally mirrors notes heard. When each spot is triggered, it gives off specific electric impulses to the brain and specific chemicals to the rest of the body, triggering emotions. So when music is heard, the two cochleas actually mirror the soundwaves heard and translate it into electricity and chemicals—you literally become what you hear. You become the movement the notes make, but it's only for the length of time the note remains audible. When the note is silenced, you stop mirroring (becoming) the sound, and it becomes memory.

By the power of imagination you metaphorically put yourself in the place of one of those sounds now gone, and come to truly, experientially know the fleetingness of life through music. When one beholds the ephemerality that is the bias of music, one becomes the dieing and so living sound of music. Music is media that engrains in you—your life's value. The value of the time you have been given to live.

What are you beholding?

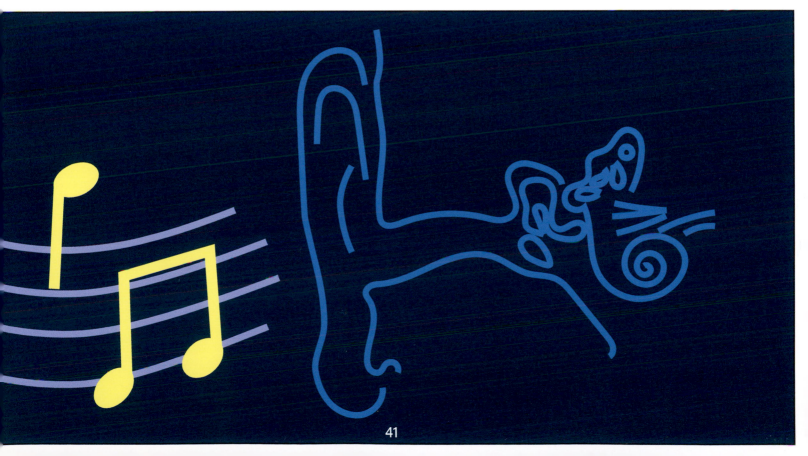

Things to behold

Live music carries most strongly the bias of ephemerality, in part because when in the setting of live music, it is often the main focus of one's attention. In a concert, the music is the main focus, which is an unusual time in and of itself because most times people are flooded with visual information, rather than purely auditory. Of course, it is precisely because live music is primarily auditory that it has the ephemeral bias most strongly.

Recorded music has this bias much less strongly, because what is recorded can be tampered with. Tampering does not necessarily mean audio engineering in post-production, but rather if the listener likes a certain part of a track they can jump straight to that moment, or repeat it over and over again—which defeats the purpose. The great moments in music are meant to be enjoyed for the brief moment they exist naturally—not in a system of control. This carries a dangerous bias of the illusion of the human's control of time, which is of course not at all true. Humanity is subject to time—it cannot be rewound, played back and controlled.

Similarly in the world of recorded music there is a hierarchy of healthy biases. Because it is much less easy to control the music playing on a vinyl than it is on a MP3 in iTunes, vinyl recordings capture much better than essence of music. It is a matter of subjecting oneself, and giving up what illusions of control humanity thinks it has over time—and microcosmically music—thus experientially, learning the value of time, through music.

Dr. David Gauger

Dr. David Gauger has had an extensive career playing trumpet with various professional orchestras including the Tulsa Philharmonic, Hong Kong Philharmonic and Chicago Symphony Orchestra. He also conducts various college symphonies and bands. His dissertation examined the relationship of music volume to the ability of people to sing along and worship, and he has done work in the ways different variables in music affect the listener.

How is music situated in a culture? How do people change in relation to music?

DG: Well what's interesting about music and all media outlets more generally is how they both reflect and create taste.

A media outlet (like a radio) will play songs that they think listeners like so that they will be listened to, which then is what is available to the listener and over time often becomes what they like, which is then reflected back onto the media outlet.

Record companies started paying off radio stations to have their songs played more for that very reason—the became cultural gatekeepers by tilting the airwaves in favor of their records. They broke into the loop of the media company reflecting and creating culture by telling them what to create more of, so that people would like it more and then buy records.

How does going to a live concert as opposed to listening to a recording change the way a person interacts with music?

DG: Why would you ever use recorded music? Well obviously there is a great difference. There is something about recorded music that is boring, in that, when it's recorded it's always perfect—the mistakes are always fixed. Perfection, even though we love to hear it, is boring. The excitement of Evel Knievel was the risk of failure—even the potential that it might all go badly brought such large crowds. The excitement of a live performance is full of danger and it communicates risk that recordings can't.

Musicians always make mistakes, and the perfection that you can engineer in the studio is not exciting—its technical and bland even though it's "perfect." But in a live performance anything could go wrong at any time, making it exciting. But there's more to it, so many layers: Risk taking is not the key to the magic of live music. Live musicians will sense what the crowd is non-verbally communicating to them—maybe they are really excited or really sad or happy—and then they will adjust how they play the music accordingly. A musician never plays the same piece twice, it's always for that audience. The pianist observes the audience and produces music in line with them, which effects the audience, which then re-informs the pianist, creating a microcosm of culture (its the same with the media outlets mentioned above.) that can only exists in live music, and that cannot exist in the sterile recorded music.

How should listeners interact with any music, live or recorded?

DG: Unfortunately people have been taught that the only valid reason for music is entertainment. This is just not true. That's like saying the only valid reason for the ability to read is so that you can read comic books.

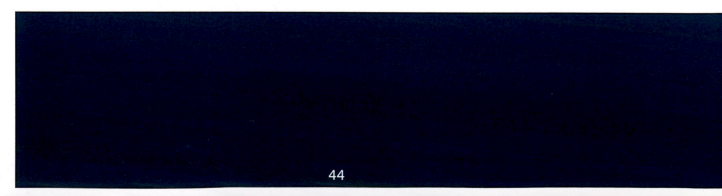

Think about it, we read for lots of reasons: signs on the road, pill bottles, encyclopedias, Shakespeare, O.Henry, E. E. Cummings—there are many different motivations to read, and you don't approach a comic book the same way as a poem. The same thing must be said of music—maybe a piece will inform some literary idea I just read, or it makes me think, makes me associate different things and make bridges. But if you're only listening to be entertained you miss out on the profundity. You're going to have a boring life.

Think about the playlist and how we can surround ourselves with only things that we like. Before the playlist you listened to what ever was on and then you'd hear it, now you can just skip what you don't like. Not only does this give us the illusion of control but also we are never forced to go outside out comfort zone. To interact with music well is all about questions. Listening to things far outside your comfort zone and asking questions and musing: how did they make that sound? Why—what does that piece mean? How did those musicians stay together? When you ask questions you start to realize how amazing it all is.

I just try to live life amazed. If you live your life in a state of amazement you'll never be bored.

THE WEIGHT OF WORDS

The decline of journalism in an ever-digital world.

Impressive

It was late one Saturday night in July of 1978, and the New York Times offices bustled to get the morning paper printed and ready to ship. An entire warehouse-sized floor of massive machines tended by bustling workers clicked and whirred like clockwork towards its inevitable printed conclusion. Tonight, though, is special- it's the last time the New York Times will be printed with big, clunky, linotype machines. The future is digital.

To get a story to press, typists transcribe that day's news on a 10-foot tall machine that eventually spits out a large block of metal containing the typed keys. Those stories are then laid out within a heavy frame and meticulously checked, then sent off to imprint a 45 pound linotype barrel that prints on the actual paper. The entire process can take hours, and each of the highly trained workers knows exactly how each machine operates in case of any technical difficulties.

Mistakes or edits cause the lengthy process to reset. Sometimes typos slip through, and the printers must repeat every single step once again, melting down and reusing the metal letters and rearranging every story. Sometimes story details get edited last minute, requiring an entire the heavy process to restart. Sometimes it can take hours.

With linotype machines, words have literal weight. The news being delivered is not a light thing, it's been meticulously edited, cautiously set, and painstakingly carried on the backs of a whole company of employees. They know the weight of words.

By July 3rd of 1978, printing goes digital and all that changes to the click of a mouse.

The 3 Functions of Journalism

1 To Inform

Since the beginning of mass communications, the primary function of journalism has been to inform groups of people about recent events or important information.

2 To Expose

Once mass communication platforms got in the hands of non government-affiliated companies and organizations, those in power needed to watch their steps—the journalists were waiting in prey to expose corruption.

3 To Analyze

A news source could report on the resignation of a corrupt governor, but if the reader doesn't comprehend the resulting power vacuum and probable flip-flop of party popularity, they aren't really informed. Journalism can often be a source of analysis for those without the time to understand every moving part.

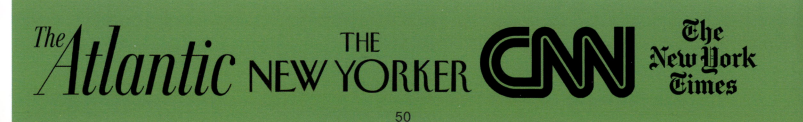

A 2013 study done by the Indiana University School of Journalism, which included over 1,000 journalistic professionals, indicated that over 60% of journalists believe their profession is headed in the wrong direction. That's six out of ten journalists that acknowledge their craft is not what they'd want it to be. The same study goes on to show that newsroom staffs are shrinking, subscriptions are dropping, and the average age of the journalist continues to increase, meaning there aren't as many young people entering the field. By journalism's own admission, things don't look good.

Through the years, journalism has gradually lost its core function as other online platforms and new mediums arise. When words weigh less, there's less thought behind them.

To understand the fall of journalism, one must first understand the function of journalism. While mediums of mass-information spreading have been around since medieval times, journalism in the traditional sense really came into its own when print became an accessible platform in the 18th century. As the profession evolved, though, three primary functions define the place of journalism. See these to the left.

> "News has migrated to a majority-online affair."

As new technologies progressed, some functions of journalism receded while others became more prominent. For example, the introduction of Twitter meant the general public could receive news from direct sources—why hear a news anchor talk about the Cubs' World Series victory when individual player accounts hosted direct quotes? This meant news sources needed to specialize in not just reporting the news, but telling readers what to think about it. An emphasis on analysis over information became a trend.

The Internet had a similar effect. When newspapers migrated from a physical product paid for through reliable subscriptions to online pages that only cost a click, news organizations lost massive revenue. Between the years 2000 and 2012, revenue from classifieds dropped by 75%, pulling a huge portion of revenue out from under agencies feet. This, combined with dropping subscription numbers, resulted in at least a 40% drop in total revenue from 2000 to 2012. News organizations began turning to online ads for a boost in revenue, sometimes allowing upwards of 4-6 ads onto a page.

News has migrated, for the most part, to a majority-online affair. With access to an entire world wide web of information, users often experience a sort of 'paralysis of choice.' If a person doesn't like the news as reported by Fox, what's stopping them from clicking over to CNN? It's not as if there are subscription fees tying them down.

At this point a peculiar shift occurred. Somewhere along the line, news organizations realized more people would click on their articles if they affirm a pre-held view. When a school shooting takes place, most Republicans would rather ingest news emphasizing the madness of the shooter, while Democrats might prefer an article detailing the methods of gun-attainment. News companies realized they can tailor their news to their audience for more secure results, and their wallets are fatter for it.

In the course of just a few years, the news world became consumerized. With the consumerization of journalism, outlets allowed themselves to report increasingly polarizing, opinionated news. The fact that most Americans believe the majority of journalism is biased proves a point—this was not the case 50 years ago.

Journalism is no longer a business built to inform. It's a business co-opted to make money.

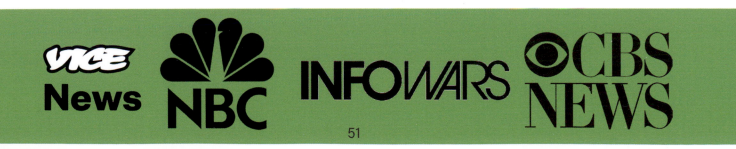

A History of Journalism

Journalism didn't lose its soul overnight—it was a gradual process that began the minute the Internet plugged into the 1990's family home. To understand how the decline came about, though, it's helpful to know how Journalism grew.

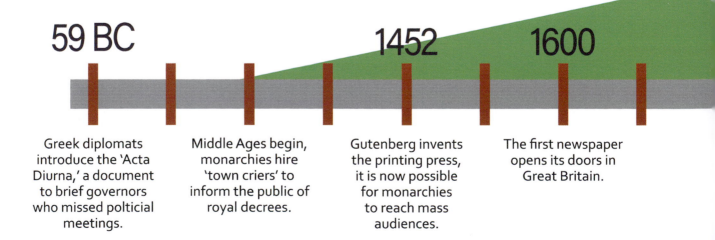

59 BC

Greek diplomats introduce the 'Acta Diurna,' a document to brief governors who missed polticial meetings.

Middle Ages begin, monarchies hire 'town criers' to inform the public of royal decrees.

1452

Gutenberg invents the printing press, it is now possible for monarchies to reach mass audiences.

1600

The first newspaper opens its doors in Great Britain.

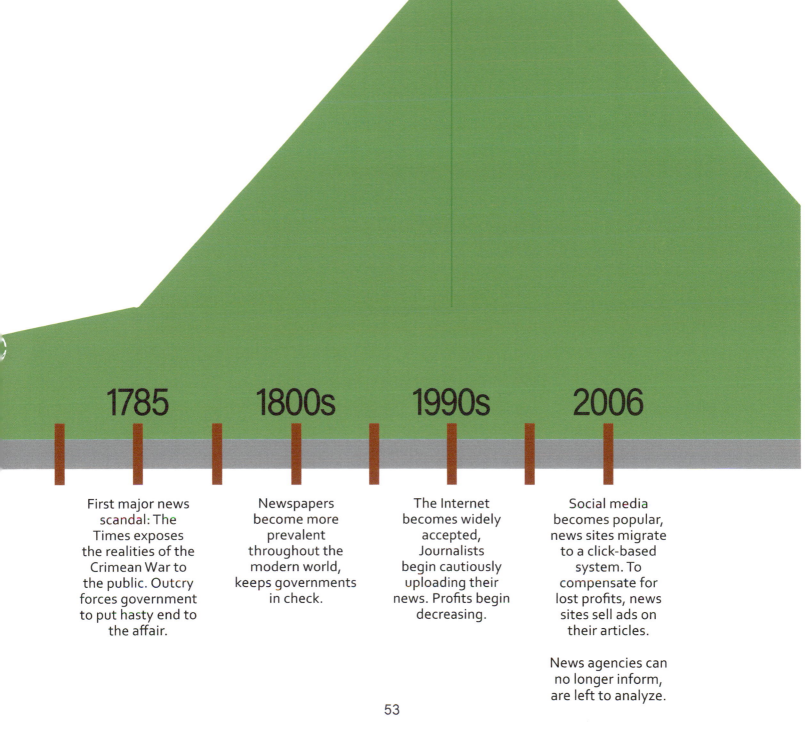

1785

First major news scandal: The Times exposes the realities of the Crimean War to the public. Outcry forces government to put hasty end to the affair.

1800s

Newspapers become more prevalent throughout the modern world, keeps governments in check.

1990s

The Internet becomes widely accepted, Journalists begin cautiously uploading their news. Profits begin decreasing.

2006

Social media becomes popular, news sites migrate to a click-based system. To compensate for lost profits, news sites sell ads on their articles.

News agencies can no longer inform, are left to analyze.

Hugo Perez was an Emmy-winning journalist in an age of rapidly evolving news. Before transitioning to advertising, Hugo spent years with NBC news as a producer and journalist, covering stories of national interest—he was even the first reporter on scene at Columbine.

When you were reporting did you notice that the introduction of the Internet platform changed journalism?

HP: One of my mentors at NBC was a producer who covered World War II and the Korean War, and I remember sitting with him many times. He would tell me how they would report on something, put it in the can, send it off with a courier, and four months later it would make air. And they had no idea if everything they said was accurate or not because they were literally in that moment alone.

The change that we were having is I could verify all my sources and I'm deep in all the materials that I was researching so it made more important the accuracy of sourcing, of being aware of other factors around the world...

I can't even imagine how much cooler it must be (today) but also dangerous because access is even more immediate. Holy smokes. Today's reporter I think are almost cheating because it's almost all predone for them, it's so easy to get information. Then they have more responsibility because when they make mistakes I think it's more a sign of intention rather omission.

(Later in the interview) I think there was an attempt by the news media to not be swayed by technology. I remember we had access to it but there was at least a semblance of wanting to hold to the ideals and truisms of what journalism was. But what happens is you stay the course and everyone else circles around you and gets more clicks than you. It doesn't matter if I'm doing great journalism if no one's watching me. You've got to kind of balance the consumerism of journalism. The world forces this to happen.

Are news agencies today blatantly biased? Is that avoidable?

HP: Unfortunately I think we're in a time where it's pretty clear where you're going to get your news. I

Hugo Perez

was talking with a friend recently about how when I studied journalism you'd learn the whole idea of a journalist being impartial. I remember I wrote a paper when I was in college about the whole concept of impartiality and how that's a false idea. By nature, being humans, we're partial to one side or the other. As a believer, as an American, as a person of a different culture, you have partiality. It is impossible to subtract yourself. As journalists, though, we were definitely taught that. [Today,] they don't teach that.

Frankly what I think it means is the consumer needs to be even more discerning. They should not take anything that's given to them at face value. You should always verify everything that you see.

As a journalist did you ever feel a tension between informing and entertaining?
HP: I feel very fortunate that I worked at a time where it felt like there was more of an emphasis on the facts. But I also worked in television news, where you've got to capture someone's attention. It was always about finding that compelling anchor to your story and then filling up the facts around them.

I would say the broader the access and opportunity journalism has gotten, the more anchored or driven by finance and power it has become.

How has the journalistic process changed?
HP: I think social media is the key. [For example,] the minute a school shooting happens, every news organization assigns their interns [to it], they probably have a protocol in place, and they start searching everything on that school. They're looking for who the kids are in the school, what are the snapchats, what are the Twitter feeds saying... And they're grabbing content left and right. That's why so quickly they identify these kids and so quickly they can build a pattern of all they said even seven years ago. It's amazing, the amount of information-

gathering that happens instantly around these kinds of things. Because of that there's an immediacy I think and so it's a little bit more dangerous. Let's say in Parkland they hadn't caught that kid right away-it might stoke his anger more to be addressed by name. I think it should add more responsibility to the coverage...

Unfortunately I think it just sensationalizes it and makes it more dramatic way faster than it probably ever has been.

If everyone has instant access to primary information, is there a need for professional journalism?
HP: I think there will always be a need for journalism because what journalism should do is give you a more complete picture and provide facts. I wish they would push impartiality stronger, but at least we still get a broader set of facts. As responsible human beings we should look to those facts and then make assessments and judgements.

Also, journalism will always have access to more official channels, like leadership and government. Journalism serves as a bully pulpit for the world and so we're able to coalesce around ideas and push. I think those things are all valuable parts of what journalism provides. And it provides a better record of the world, too.

What's your opinion on the current state of journalism?
HP: I'm saddened that it's become so fragmented and so personality and opinion driven. I have many friends that are still journalists whom I respect and appreciate their approaches... I just think the rise of social and digital and the need for instant gratification has changed the ability to report on a story the way it should be reported. It saddens me, and I don't know how we grab it back.

THE MEDIA OF FINDING OUT

How techniques of finding answers
shape and influence learning endeavors.

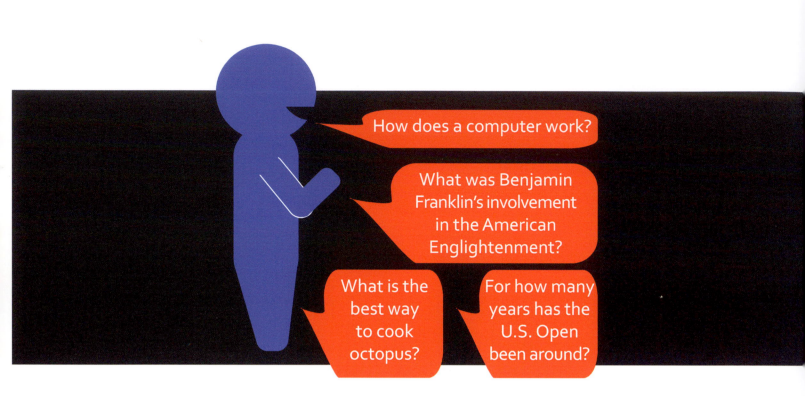

The question-answering genies in pockets and homes are convenient, immediate, and offer access to an endless database of various perspectives. However, daily engagement with "Google as teacher" actually limit the way the questioning brain functions.

Ironically, learning information through a search engine limits the way a person can learn information.

Searching Google, asking Siri, or summoning Alexa structures the experience of finding things out by removing the difficulty, in turn destroying the possibility for developing learning skills. Against these various digital means of finding out, alternative media must also be examined and juxtaposed. One of these alternative resources is investigation through the codex.

(That means reading a book.)

The medium of communication has an important and often overlooked role to play in influencing the communicated message, through the structure inherent to that medium. So how do the modes and methods we use to figure things out, to learn information, and to engage curiosity on an everyday basis, influence learning experiences?

Reading an actual book to answer a question facilitates greater opportunity for learning and the development of learning skills for the future. As with all media, the way an experience is structured by a medium must not be overlooked or under-evaluated. Instead, every medium must undergo thorough and even cautious evaluation before it is to be trusted and integrated.

The modern world is saturated with information. The title given by many as the defining force of our time in history is "the information age." With so much knowledge available to us, a fundamental question appears: How should we go about finding things out, so as to best shape our learning abilities?

If the "commodity" within the "market" of the information age is fact, knowledge, or know-how, then the ability to learn and to learn well is foundationally the force that gives us "fitness" within this environment, in the Darwinian sense. Those who adapt most appropriately to fit within an environment are those who survive. The environmental demand in the information age is, simply put, "Know!" The question then, of how we pursue learning, is paramount to survival in the information age. Through understanding the psychology behind our mental learning endeavors, we can gain a sense of how we ought to gather information in a way that fosters true learning. Doing so is nothing short of giving oneself the ability to "survive," which translated from Darwinian language, is to dominate.

The following is a brief examination of some elements that can lead to true and lasting learning, according to Anita Woolfolk and Kay Margetts' book, "Educational Psychology." While Woolfolk and Margetts are focused on education proper, their values can and should be understood and implemented in the discussion of the methods of informal everyday learning as well. Chapter seven, *Cognitive Views of Learning* lays out "A recent cognitive science model of the information processing system" and describes the model below:

Information is encoded in sensory memory, where perception and attention determine what will be held in working memory for further use... Thoroughly processed and connected information becomes part of long-term memory, and when activated again, becomes part of working memory. Implicit memories are formed without conscious effort . . . Attention has a role in all three memory processes and in the interactions among them.

Through the development of working memory into long-term memory, attention and perception are identified as key elements for solidifying information into the brain in a lasting way. Attention is a key in the interplay. This is no novel concept—common knowledge supports the notion that the more we attend to something, the higher level of engagement we will have, and the greater the personal gain will be. Later we read, "Attention takes effort and is a limited resource." Focused effort in any endeavor leads to a greater reward. Woolfolk and Margetts state, "Understanding is more than memorising. It is more than retelling in your own words. Understanding involves complex thinking skills for appropriately transforming and using knowledge, skills, and ideas."

Understanding—the substance of learning—requires not only attention, but a complex engagement of a topic or an idea. It includes the ability to apply the knowledge gained in various ways. These endeavors require effort and careful attention—a pursuit which implies intentionality in creating the appropriate space and time for the process.

How does the smartphone search engage with these elements of learning? Because of the immediacy and ease of the five-second answer gained from Google searching, effort and attention can be greatly reduced in the process of "finding out." Then there is the aspect of the narrow focus of this digital process. Through the vastness and searchable

A working model of learning

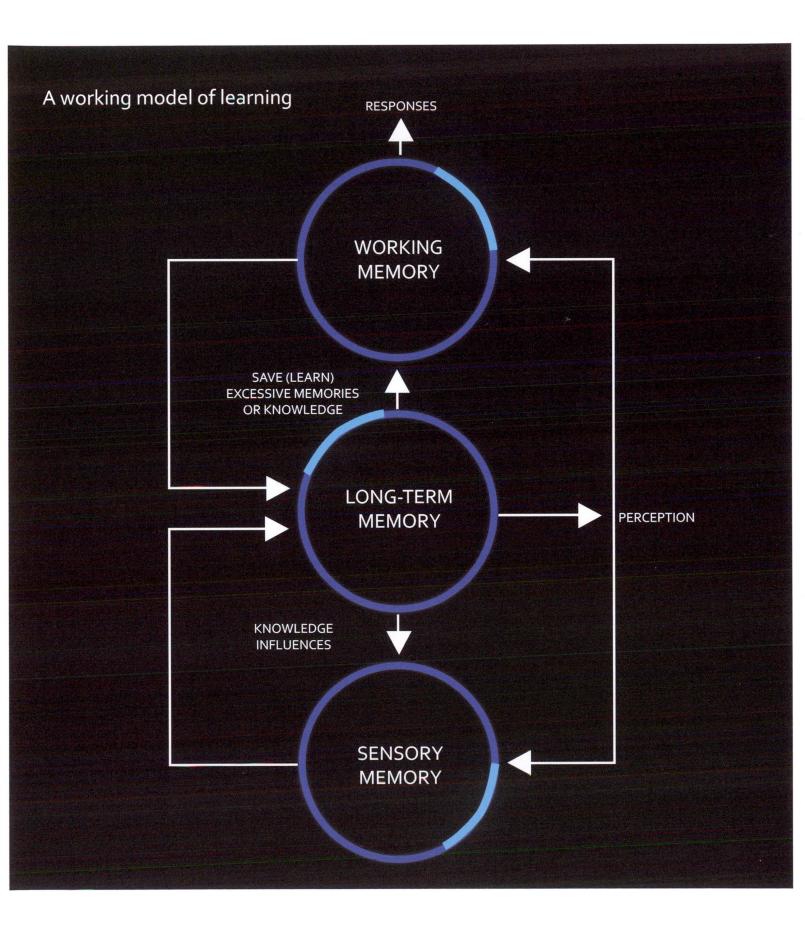

nature of the Internet, questions can be answered, in most cases, exactly as they have been asked. A brief example: In visiting a couple's home recently, I had the joy of not only being hosted by Justin and Morgan, but by Alexa as well. Many times throughout the night Alexa or Google answered questions that we asked. "What is a Green Beret?" When the question came up in our dialogue, the brief and exact summarized Internet answer followed soon after. The brevity of the search and specificity of the answer did not create the space for the question to gain any meaningful or memorable context in the short time before it was answered, nor in the even shorter time that we discussed it after the search results came in.

Our Internet search allowed for a lost opportunity. We did not learn the context around our question and the body of knowledge surrounding its answer. We also lost an opportunity to creatively explore the curiosity that comes from having the question unanswered. Before we turned to the Internet, different people in the room made suggestions on what we thought the answer might be. We engaged our curiosity, and discussed various aspects of the topic. But, once we got our one-line answer, the conversation soon died. That was it. Now that we knew, there was no longer any point in the discussion.

There is no longer room to explore a question before it is answered, if an answer is always immediate. It is important to realize that the smartphone search does not necessitate the limiting effects of learning. However, the structure of smartphone-searching does allow for such dangers, and the mere allowance of dangers must be taken seriously. Now consider if at that dinner party, we had pursued an alternative to the Google search: reading a book on the matter. This is a tedious, old, and often frustratingly slow way of learning information on an everyday basis. Unlike the Google search, it takes much more effort to go through the process of finding a book on green berets, getting our hands on it, and then finding the space to read it. Even if it is a simple search in an encyclopedia, it still requires patience until we could get to an encyclopedia and begin the search. A book requires wading through, which often results in a more context-driven understanding of a topic. It is the kind of searching that requires a higher level of attention and focus, even to do half-heartedly, in comparison to Internet searching. It is done on its own—it demands space and time for a search—and is not an easy option for the multitasker. It demands attention from the reader. All of these structural necessities encourage careful attention, effort, time, space, complex thinking, and provide a vast context to the subject at hand.

> "*Understanding* includes the ability to apply the knowledge."

This effort and attentiveness can at first be tiresome and challenging, but leads to a depth of knowledge on the topic of inquiry. Book research creates literacy, insources (rather than outsources) the research process, trains the mind, and creates a memorable event. Alexa's voice leaves the mind as quickly as it enters.

Through media analysis, the fact becomes strikingly clear that the use of different methods and means of finding things out structures learning in vastly different ways. While universal value claims on media as they holistically influence us are difficult, specific aspects of each medium can and should be judged as helpful or hurtful to our own personal learning endeavors.

Other Media of Finding Out

Watching a documentary

Encourages: waiting until you can watch the film, and pondering the subject until then. It also encourages a dramatic understanding of the subject, authored by creators who want to tell a compelling story, and who have likely done a fair amount of research. Requires a minimum of an hour worth of your time, which requires some level of deeper interest.

Dangers: because of the entertainment aspect of film, viewers may be less critical, engaged, and attentive than is needed for long lasting learning.

Internet Wikis

Encourages: a deeper investigation than a Google search, which requires more commitment to an investigation. It takes all your attention, and a set apart time, along with more reputable and well-researched sources than a basic Google search can offer.

Dangers: even this use of the Internet can tempt towards a "grab and go" style of finding things out, and can exclude valuable context that is crucial to further and deeper learning.

Asking a friend

Encourages: finding the right person to ask through a process of social interactions; a healthy practice of using your social resources around you to grow in learning. It will likely allow you to understand the person's level of expertise on the matter based on their response. Also, this endeavor will allow you to explore various other questions around the subject that they encourage you to explore, as well as the sources where they have learned the knowledge at hand.

Dangers: asking a individual about a subject that they have been misinformed on can perpetuate a cycle of misinformation.

Trial and Error

Encourages: the value of the personal journey of testing personal ideas on a matter in the world. It can strengthen curiosity, and allow ample room to explore not only the answer to a question, but the value of the question itself. Trial and error can lead to a more experiential knowledge of the truth of a matter, that is deeper than getting information from an outside source

Dangers: intentionally avoiding outside sources for information can create a "reinventing the wheel" situation that does not lead to personal growth in the same way that using the expertise around you might be able to.

Kenneth Trotter

Kenneth Trotter is a career educator who founded Trinitas Christian School in Pensacola, Florida, and Christ Classical School in San Louis Obispo, California. Learning is kinda his thing.

What role does method or medium play in the education process?
KT: The first and foundational question we ask is, "how does a student learn?" The best teaching methodology is one that utilizes the way a child learns, that teaches "with the grain" of their development, and adjusts with the various changes in the education process.

What are the ways mature students, or adults, learn?
KT: The learning process consists of three stages: learning the grammar of a thing, learning the logic of it, and finally developing a rhetoric of the thing that engage the grammar and logic of it.

What is the role of attention in education?
KT: Too often people only hear what information they need, but they have not listened. To be attentive is to be present, actively focused, and engaged. You cannot learn if you are not attentive.

How does technology affect education?
KT: We must believe that technology *can* enhance attentiveness, but there is a form of entertainment attached to screens. This results in digital technology probably having an overall adverse effect learning. We have conditioned ourselves towards such a high level of stimulus in our lives, that the low level of stimulus within the educational environment is unacceptable to us. We have reduced learning to simple information exchange, and have lost the learning depth that accompanies carefully reading a book.

PRESENCE

How tech that promises connection delivers separation.

Waiting for the traffic light to change, the elevator doors to open, or for a late coffee date are all now considered appropriate instances to fill time with digital technology. First thoughts of, "What have I missed out on? Whose 'likes' have I not been notified of yet? Did my boss email me back?" soon turn into questions of, "Where am I? What am I doing? What was the task at hand?"

Not only do we now create habits of filling any free moment with these welcomed digital distractions, they also hinder our relationships. M.I.T. professor Sherry Turkle says that mobile devices promise an ability to "slip in and out of wherever you are to be wherever you want to be, with no social stigma [creating] a new set of social mores that allow for a split attention in human relationships and human community... I really couldn't say 'Oh, excuse me' and just open up a book in the middle of a conversation."

What is missed in relationships and in real time should be considered by those who seek to be connected to reality and not just the virtual. When the phone call ends and the screen turns black, are we just then tuning into the history happening in real time before our eyes? Today, society chooses to commune with the virtual rather than the real... with the almost but not quite... with technology instead of people.

In withdrawing to what has become more comfortable, the technological man more comfortably connects through screens rather than by human interaction. Although these practices are thought of as a more normalized behavior, to choose the phone over the person in company has negative effects on all parties.

Technology promises connection—it is easy to believe this claim at face value. But in reality, technology puts up walls and separates others.

For example, FaceTime is not reality. Just ask any long distance couple and they will emphatically agree that to be connected on a screen is nothing compared to being truly together. The virtual experience of FaceTime is only a reflection of reality—it is a disembodied experience. Since video captures image, movement and sound, the manipulated senses can make FaceTime seem more real than a phone call or a written letter.

The same is true for any media with the inherent bias of displacement and manipulation of multiple senses (such as Snapchat, Instagram and Facebook). As soon as one believes the mediated moving images are equivalent to "being together," one no longer values an embodied communal reality.

All senses—sound, sight, smell, touch, and taste are available and in play when in person. Yet only a few are available through mediated channels of varying technologies.

The long distance couple longs to be together in person, but they settle for digital connection while apart. They resort to connection through the screen only because they cannot have embodied reality. However, society now conforms to the screen even while physically with others, thus choosing to look into their private screens instead of into each other's eyes. Research shows that people are happier when they are present—this being a physical and mental presence. It is completely possible to be bodily present yet mentally absent.

This phenomenon of common occurrence has officially been named phubbing (phone + snubbing). Not only is it impolite behavior to give attention to a smartphone instead of present company (whether it be acquaintances, friends, family or a significant other), there are also proven detrimental effects. Placing a higher importance to the content of one's phone (whether it is a sleeping puppy on Instagram, a message from another friend, or a new green bean casserole recipe) communicates to the present human company that they are less important—that they are worth less—than the phone. The scrolling can wait, but the relationships with the present company should not have to.

Similarly, when one feels awkward when interrupting a friend who is scrolling on their phone, they exhibit an understanding that they value the technology over the human. Simply put, their actions prove a value for the virtual over reality. This points to the conclusion that society is now more comfortable with machine than with their dinner date. Even when one is with others engaging in human conversation, he may excuse himself so that he can text.

Phubbing is cyclical, meaning the more that people choose to gaze at their phone instead of commune with the people around them, the more that behavior is adopted and reciprocated. To the opposite effect, the more face-to-face human interaction is favored rather than the virtual when together, the less people will feel an urge to be on their phones. Meredith E. David and James A. Roberts explain social effects of phubbing in their 2017 study, *Phubbed and Alone: Phone Snubbing, Social Exclusion, and Attachment to Social Media*. Their research shows that when people are snubbed by their company for a phone, they are likely to desire attention—through social media. David and Roberts state,

"As humans, we have an innate desire to belong, to receive attention, and to feel appreciated. The social awards of attention and praise are particularly relevant to our desire for social connection. Thus, it is posited that phubbing creates a sense of social exclusion that increases an individual's need for attention or to belong. People are continually monitoring their levels of inclusion and will divert their attention resources to opportunities to connect with others when their sense of inclusion drops below an acceptable level... in an effort to restore a desired level of belonging, phubbed individuals may turn to their phones and actively engage with social media to regain the sense of social inclusion threatened by other's phubbing."

Simply put, social interactions are inhibited by the very technologies that have promised advancements.

In her TED talk "Connected, but alone?" Sherry Turkle elegantly says, "We are smitten with technology, and we are afraid like young lovers that too much talking might spoil the romance. But it's time to talk."

> "It is completely possible to be bodily present yet mentally absent."

Can You Even?

Take this quiz to see if you're missing out on life in exchange for staying connected.

	Yes	No
I feel more relaxed and comfortable when communicating through edited texts than in person.	☐	☐
I feel irrelevant without posting status updates and pictures to be "present" through social media.	☐	☐
I often feel like I'm missing out on experiences I see via social media.	☐	☐
I feel jealous when I see posts from other people's life via social media.	☐	☐
I feel left out and/or anxious when I'm not able to check social media updates.	☐	☐
I text my family when I'm with my friends, but then text my friends when I'm with my family.	☐	☐
It's easier to to text someone an especially uncomfortable, difficult, or bold message instead of telling them in person. (Think of when you told your first crush you liked them . . . was it to their face?)	☐	☐

Christina Crook

Christina Crook, author of *The Joy of Missing Out: Finding Balance in a Wired World* is a wife and mother living in Toronto, Canada. She is a graduate of the Simon Fraser University School of Communication, and often speaks and writes on the topic of technology and human relationships.

Why did you write *The Joy of Missing Out*?

CC: I had a growing uneasiness for a couple of years. I moved from the west coast British Columbia to Toronto, and all my relationships were mediated by technology since my family and friends were not there. I noticed that my relationships were beginning to lack because of the mediation. Plus, there were some people that I could not check in with on Facebook, and I was growing more uncomfortable with that. So, I decided to take a break from the Internet for 31 days. During each of those days, I wrote a letter on my old typewriter and sent them to one particular friend.

In your experience with this topic, what are some responses you have from others?

CC: People have been very receptive to my book and ideas, since it hits at the core of our needs as humans—we desire to connect in a meaningful way. "Social" channels enable us to do so, but it is limited. Since over 80% of communication is nonverbal, communication through text misses out on the body language and voice. When I mention this during speaking engagements, people nod their heads with great enthusiasm. The problem is that instead of performing one function, like for an alarm clock, our devices now serve so many needs that we use everyday—this can be 100, or maybe 500 uses in one device—and we cannot picture living without them.

Have any of your views toward technology changed since writing your book?

CC: My views have not changed as much since writing the book as they did in the process of writing it. Kevin Kelly, the cofounder of Wired Magazine, says the Amish do not reject all technology at hand, but rather, they have questions to run it through, such as "is this technology good for the soul? Is it good for community?" Kevin's article states:

1) They are selective. They know how to say "no" and are not afraid to refuse new things. They ban more than they adopt.
2) They evaluate new things by experience instead of by theory. They let the early adopters get their jollies by pioneering new stuff under watchful eyes.
3) They have criteria by which to select choices: technologies must enhance family and community and distance themselves from the outside world.
4) The choices are not individual, but communal. The community shapes and enforces technological direction.

Similarly, I think as Christians we should ask, "Is this technology enlivening my relationship with God? With others?"

How do we become more human in an increasingly technological world?

CC: *Laughs* This is THE question. I would say we need to look for opportunities to be human. Seek out opportunities to become fully present to the world. Since it is really easy to hide in online spaces, it is increasingly scary for people to engage with the real world when people are used to control found in online spaces. We push ourselves to step outside of what is comfortable, which is also completely within the Christian ethic. We are to minister to the poor, including the poor in spirit.

How do we relate to people in a more whole and fulfilling way today?

CC: Vulnerability begets vulnerability. If we are not vulnerable, people will not be either. It is becoming more and more truly Herculean to choose to go out and be with people rather than stay at home and communicate online and watch Netflix. We become deeply embedded in those habits. So when people scroll through their Instagram page to see an endless amount of seemingly perfect pictures and posts, then sees a vulnerable post, I would encourage people to make a direct touch point. Whether that is through email, a phone call, or meeting in person if that is possible, because the more direct we can be with people, the more connected we will be, full stop.

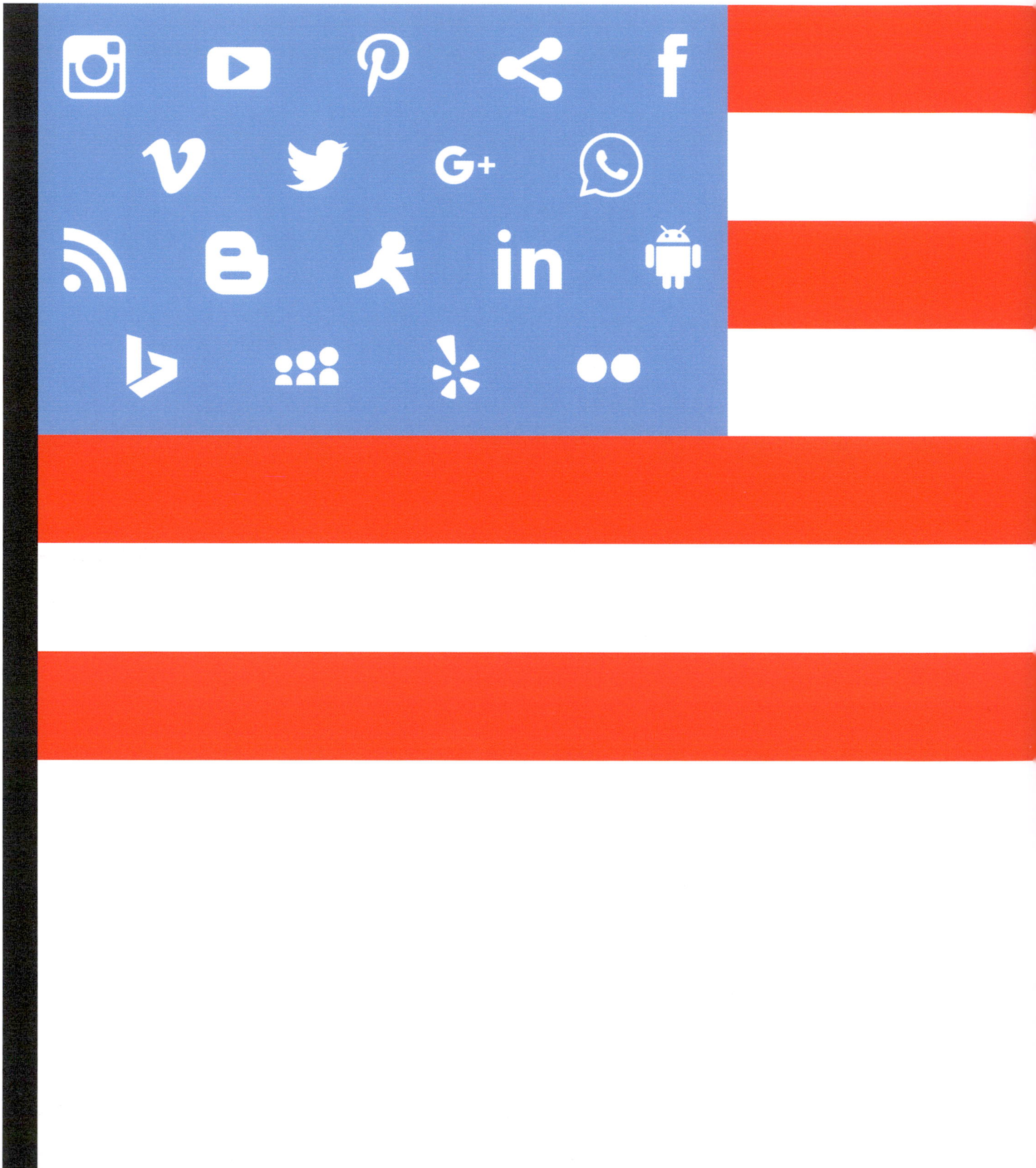

MEDIA AS METAPHOR

The rise of personality politics in a social media America.

Social media has changed Politics.

The scene is a small suburban living room, as the later hours of the evening creep in on the expectant adults. Dinner is eaten, dishes are cleaned, and husband and wife sit on the couch after a long day at work. They power on the television to their favorite show—in this episode, the main characters are lined on a stage in order of importance—squabbling and spectacle ensue. The Presidential Debate has begun.

Today, modern politics in the United States may be better described as a reality tv show for fifth graders than a public forum about the next leader of the free world. Candidates tweet out hit pieces at their enemies, brag about hand size, and storm out of auditoriums when things don't go their way. While once a rational discussion about the future of the United States of America, politics has become more about drama than doctrine.

American politics didn't devolve for no reason, though. Politicians didn't randomly decide to take a page from the Survivor playbook—it was a gradual transformation due to the rise of television, the Internet, and social media. After all, it was only 2008 when no major candidate had their own Instagram or Twitter account. Today, tax reform can be summed up in 140 characters, no language is too base for candidates, and publicity stunts are par for the course.

Today, bad politics makes for great entertainment.

Actual advertisements for the presidential debate better resemble the next Pay-per-View match.

Reality TV politics is no surprise to famed Media Ecology prophet Neil Postman. In the fourth chapter of his landmark book *Amusing Ourselves to Death*, a manifesto about entertainment-media's effect on the Western world, he asserts that technology has an irreversible impression on society. To Postman, a society's citizens will mold and fit the form of media most cherished in their society, a concept he calls 'media as metaphor.' Whatever form of media the masses are most literate in, Postman says, is a metaphor of that culture.

As an example, Neil Postman cites the numerous well-documented debates held by Abraham Lincoln and rival Stephen Douglas. Because the written book reigned as the dominant media, these debates tended to last upwards of seven hours, and often saw immense crowd participation. At these events, the language spoken was the language of print culture. Before officially beginning one of his speeches, Lincoln said the following simply to imply he might run out of speaking time:

"It will readily occur to you that I cannot; in half an hour, notice all the things that so able a man as Judge Douglas can say in an hour and a half' and I hope, therefore, if there be anything that he has said upon which you would like to hear something from me, but which I omit to comment upon, you will bear in mind that it would be expecting an impossibility for me to cover his whole ground."

In a Twitter dominated world, it's difficult to imagine any person, even one in the highest office in the country, speaking with such intellect or humility. Postman muses that even if a modern president were to speak in such manner, his audience probably wouldn't understand him. The buzzword-laden, lowest common denominator state of modern politics proves Postman's prophetic observance.

How then, did politics transform into what it is today? Perhaps the first sign of this shift came when politics migrated from radio to television. The first televised presidential debate aired alongside its radio counterpart in 1960, a showdown between Republican Richard Nixon and Democrat John F. Kennedy. Politics would never be the same again.

After the debate most radio listeners found Nixon the winner—he was calm, clear, and rational. TV viewers, though, could clearly point to Kennedy as the winner, by a landslide. The well-dressed looks of Kennedy impressed the viewing public, while the apparent frumpiness of Nixon (who had just been released from the hospital) turned viewers off. When the dominant media of America became television, Americans suddenly needed an attractive president.

This event marks a definitive shift in the way politics are handled, and specifically, candidates are chosen. No longer are candidates the embodiments of ideals and policies an American voter may support, no longer does their appeal lie solely in what they can do for their country's citizens. After the marriage of TV and politics, a candidate's popularity lies in their personality, looks, mannerisms, and even jokes. When politics was introduced to the television, politics became Hollywoodized.

Politics remained a TV event for decades, but something unique had occurred by the 2016 election—the introduction of social media. Though a few candidates had used Facebook in the past two races, 2016 marked the point where a robust social media suite was all but required to contend. By 2016, social media had replaced television as the dominant form of entertainment-media. Politics would never be the same again. This change had serious ramifications for candidate behavior even off their social media platforms.

Media is metaphor. When a society adopts a new form of media—radio, television, social platforms—it irreversibly transforms to reflect the values of that media. The same principle applies to a society's politics. When society values only those social media celebrities, its politicians morph to fit the mold.

That actually Happened

The 2016 election had a lot going on, with almost too many candidates to account for and wild antics on each side. The presidential shenanigans exemplify politicians rising to give the entertainment-hungry society what it demands. Here are some things that actually happened in the 2016 election.

Candidates pander to their core audience.

Donald J. Trump
@realDonaldTrump
Follow

The media and establishment want me out of the race so badly - I WILL NEVER DROP OUT OF THE RACE, WILL NEVER LET MY SUPPORTERS DOWN! #MAGA

12:40 PM - 8 Oct 2016

38,538 Retweets 99,051 Likes

28K   39K   99K

Hillary Clinton
@HillaryClinton
Follow

How does your student loan debt make you feel?
Tell us in 3 emojis or less.

11:49 AM - 12 Aug 2015

7,251 Retweets 6,210 Likes

8.4K   7.3K   6.2K

News footage of a painting in Ben Carson's home airs to large news coverage.

TOGETHER.

Bernie Sanders capitalizes on a stray bird that landed on his podium during a campaign.

"He is a war hero because he was captured," Trump said, cutting him off. "I like people that weren't captured, OK? I hate to tell you. He is a war hero because he was captured. OK, you can have -- I believe perhaps he is a war hero."

"And, he referred to my hands—'if they're small, something else must be small.' I guarantee you there's no problem. I guarantee."

-President Donald Trump

Ted Cruz demonstrates to audience how to cook bacon with a machine gun.

Dr. Michael McDuffee

Dr. Michael McDuffee is an author and speaker on historical Christianity and politics, and a professor at the Moody Bible Institute in Chicago. He's a thinker, a poet, and a Christian. Here are his thoughts.

What is unique about American politics?

MM: Some of the characteristics unique to America is our sense of American exceptionalism, that the United States is some kind of ordained vessel of God and that God is a synchronistic God made up of the Bible is one part, the enlightenment, and romantic sentimentalism as another. This is the God that we serve through American Civil Religion, who bestows upon us a chosen status. And we have a sense of identity through living out that chosen status. And I don't care if you're on the left and the chosen status appoints you to execute justice upon the world or if you're on the right and that chosen status has called to execute freedom upon the world.

The key thing is that from an American point of view, this false god in whom we trust has given us this mandate. It's a surrogate, a great commission to go out into the world and teach all the nations, making them disciples of either freedom or justice in accordance with the American way. Even today, we can see this in the contemporary two party system where one is saying, 'let's make America great again,' which means let's go back to a traditional set of values in order to fulfill this mandate of the false god of American civil religion. The other side says, 'No, no, no, no. We have to continue the secular scientific humanitarian agenda in order to fulfill the mandate of the same God for purposes of justice.

How have you seen the political scene in America change for the past two to three elections?

MM: Each cycle we see a decline in the power of parties and the growing power of personality cults. It's much more an issue of marketing and branding than it is an issue about issues, as they used to be a party platforms.

There used to be speeches of substance. There used to be a far more textually oriented kind of a life and time. People had the patience to listen, to read, to reflect and debate. We don't have that time now. We have been cattle prodded into a much more compressed sense of time. As one scholar put it, where we are living in the future. Now everything is now.

Of course, social media is an accelerant of that. And it's amazing. We can see that we're interacting out of time with our own cells because of how often things that have been texted by very intelligent people in powerful places nonetheless have content that make the author (think) "I've got to retract that. I've got to erase that…"

We are literally addicting ourselves to technology that is robbing us of the richness of giving thought to what we're saying. So you have that combined with personality cult- we're allowing ourselves to be channeled into a way of life that is far more controlled, managed, policed, than we should. It's destructive. Do people converse with one another over ideas of substance? Maybe.

How do Christians respond?

MM: Christians are not to fall into despair over this, and we're not to withdraw. Jesus is Lord. Christians are to proclaim him in the public square. But the public square always has been local. That's where the public square is. Years ago, a speaker of the house when Reagan was president, Tip O'Neill, said, all politics is local. Well, that's a very biblical thought. We are ambassadors of Christ and the embassy through which we work is our local church.

But we've drank the Kool-Aid for the past 40 years—we think the only way you bring about change is through control. To gain control, you have to garner the money and you get organized and you've got to secure a voting block on a national level… What has that given us since the 1970s? Since evangelicals have [been] politically engaged the whole idea was to legislate the values that are grounded in Scripture to assure the common good of American society… We're worse off now.

All good Christian politics is local politics. Any good that comes out of politics on a national level from a Christian perspective will always be rooted in and be fruit of local engagement. Wow. Wow.

Where do you see American politics the next election?

MM: I'm not surprised and it's reflective of what people are running through the veins of their soul every night, watching whatever. It's where we are. It's not like he's an outlier, he's no different than where the culture is. I have no idea what's going to happen. I have no idea what kind of candidates we will have because of him having been elected. The brackets have shifted. That's all I know. And I tell you what, if the game of baseball changed at the rate that politics have changed through these past two administrations, then fans in the stands would have no idea what it is and wouldn't have a clue as to what's the score.

Credits

Writers

Rachel Armamentos
Defining a Technological Society
The Medium is the Message
Addicted by Design
Presence

Brock Lockenour
The Medium is the Message
The Weight of Words
Media as Metaphor

Ryan Snyder
You Become What You Behold

Tim Holland
The Media of Finding Out

Layout Design

Brock Lockenour

Graphic Artists

Kaylee Lockenour
You Become What You Behold
The Media of Finding Out

Song Kim
Addicted by Design

Special Thanks

Brian Kammerzelt,
Read Mercer Schuchardt,
Eric McLuhan,
Eric Brende,
David Gauger,
Hugo Perez,
Kenneth Trotter,
Christina Crook,
Michael McDuffee,

And many more.

Other Media Usage:

All images of people are used by permission from the person.
Mountains and Cars in Technological Society - Freepik

Rachel Armamentos:

Rachel seeks to find joy in everyday wonders, enjoys bringing people together in genuine community, and is always happiest at the beach. Her interest in the study of media ecology is founded on a passion for people and the desire for a better understanding of the environment that is created by the media we live in. She plans to further her education with a study of theology and media ecology.

Brock Lockenour:

Brock Lockenour makes stuff. Find him @brock.locke on Instagram or at brocklockenour.com

Contact Info:

rachelsuz15@gmail.com
brocklockenour@gmail.com